Tree of Light

A Christmas musical for the church
that enjoys exuberant worship!

Created and Arranged by
Dale Mathews and Michael Frazier

Orchestrated by Michael Frazier

As Recorded by The Lee College Campus Choir, Director: Dr. David Horton
Narration Written by Dale Evrist: Senior Pastor, New Song Christian Fellowship

Also Available:

C3230N	Listening Cassette
TR3230C	Stereo Track Accompaniment Cassette
TRS3230C	Split-Track Accompaniment Cassette
TRS3230CD	Split-Track Accompaniment CD
C3230S	Soprano Rehearsal Cassette
C3230A	Alto Rehearsal Cassette
C3230T	Tenor Rehearsal Cassette
C3230B	Bass Rehearsal Cassette
OR3230	Orchestration
CS3230	Conductor's Score
CBK3230	Preview Pak
P3230	Posters
BU3230	Bulletins

Instrumentation:

Flute 1,2
Oboe
Trumpet 1,2,3
French Horn 1,2
Trombone 1,2,3,4
Harp
Percussion 1,2
Violin 1,2
Viola
Cello
Contra Bass
Rhythm

Substitute Parts:
Clarinet
Alto/Tenor Sax

BRENTWOOD
MUSIC
PUBLISHING

CONTENTS

Joy To The World

Arranged by Michael Frazier and Dale Mathews

4

* JOY TO THE WORLD (Janet McMahan Wilson, Dale Mathews)

Joy to the world,___ He has giv-en us a Sav-
He rules the world,___ He rules o-ver all the na-

Db   Ab   Db   Db   Db/Ab

47

ior,___ Joy to the world,___ the
tions,___ He rules the world___ with

Ab   Db   Ab   Db   Db/F   Gb

50

Lord is come;___ Hosts of heav-en give Him glo-
truth and grace;___ We re-joice in our sal-va-

Db/Ab   Ab   Db/F   Gb   Ab/Gb

ry, we re - joice___ in their song,___
tion, through the gift of God's own Son,___

Joy to the world___ the Lord is come!___

(page 8, measure 44)

na - ture sing.___ And heav - en and

heav - en___ and na - ture

sing.___

Wonderful Counselor

Words and Music by
WAYNE GOODINE
Arranged by Michael Frazier

NARRATOR: On the night that Jesus was born, an angel of the Lord, shrouded in the blaze of God's glorious light, appeared to startled shepherds and declared to them "good news of great joy." This joyous news was that the light and life of God had come into the world in the person of God's Son; born as a Baby, in a little town called Bethlehem.

This truly was wonderful news for people everywhere. For their spiritual lives were dead and darkened. They had become weary, discouraged and hopeless. They were unable to experience the reality of a vital relationship with the living God.

But God, because of His great love for man *(Music starts.)* and because of His desire for man to know Him intimately, sent Jesus to lead people out of darkness

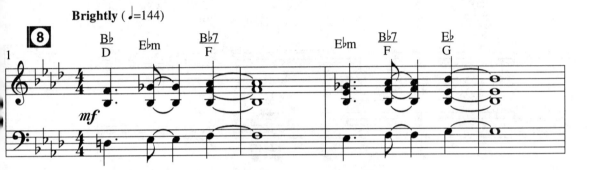

and into His marvelous light. That is the heart of the message of Christmas.

That the light of truth and hope has dawned for all who will receive it.

He shall be called a Friend to the friend - less and
Je - sus is His name.

2. I-

71
18
Prince of Peace,
My Ev-er - last - ing Fa - ther,
Je - sus!
Je - sus!
F♭/A♭
G♭/A♭
74
Je - sus!
Je - sus!
Je - sus!
Je - sus!
F♭/A♭
G♭/A♭

24

91

called: Em- man - u -el, God with us, King of

Eb F/Eb Dm7 Gm7

93

Kings, for - ev -er the same, He shall be

Cm7 F7 Bb Cm/Bb Bb

95

called a Friend to the friend - less and

Eb D7 F/G Gm7

Beautiful Name Underscore

Music by
MICHAEL FRAZIER
Arranged by Michael Frazier

NARRATOR: *(Music Starts.)* "...Call His name Jesus." God sent an angel to Joseph, Jesus' earthly father, to say those very words to him.

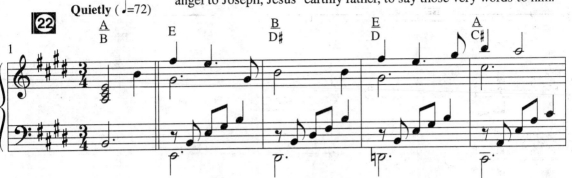

To tell Him exactly what name He wanted this baby to have. It had to be a name that would communicate clearly His purpose for coming to live among men.

So the angel said to name Him Jesus, which literally means "Savior, Healer, Deliverer," because His reason for coming

was to gloriously liberate people from the power of sin in their lives. To give them a new life and a new beginning, as His new creation, destined for high purpose in Him.

Beautiful Name Medley

Arranged by Michael Frazier and Dale Mathews

NARRATOR: He had come to proclaim good news of God's great love *(Music starts.)* and then to share that love not only as a Savior, but also as a friend. For those of us who

know Him and who have experienced His grace and His love, we know of no more beautiful name than the name of our Savior and our friend, Jesus.

* THAT BEAUTIFUL NAME (Perry, Camp)

1. I know of a name, a
(2. I) know of a name, a

* WE'LL CALL HIM JESUS (Karen Dean)

sin.   His name is

Je - sus,   Je - sus,   Je - sus!

NARRATOR: Thank you Jesus. Thank you for all that you are to us: our Savior, our King, our Lord and our Friend.

We adore you Jesus and we're not ashamed to lift up your great name. For you alone are
worthy of all glory, honor, and praise.

* COME, LET US ADORE HIM (Dale Mathews)
(Congregation may join 2nd time)

Come, let us a-dore___ Him, Come, bow down be-

fore___ Him, Come, let us wor-ship Him,

Jesus, What A Wonderful Child

TRADITIONAL
Arranged by Michael Frazier

44

(page 42, meas. 5)

73

molto rit.

Glo - ry,   glo - ry,   glo - ry to the new -

A
E

E
D

A
C#

Bm A#°7

B7(♭9)

molto rit.

76

rit.

Fine

born ___   King! _____

E+   E7

A

rit.

79

Reprise 〔45〕 *(no other ID's on reprise)*

D.S.
(page 48, meas.57)

D
E

Drum fill

3

Silent Night

Words by JOSEPH MOHR
Music by FRANZ GRUBER
Arranged by Michael Frazier

NARRATOR: What an incredible moment that must have been when the angels rang out with cries of "Glory to God in the highest and on earth, peace, goodwill toward men." It was a heavenly celebration that heralded the birth of the most wonderful, remarkable child that was ever born. A child who was the King of Kings and the Lord of Lords. A child that would change the destiny of mankind forever.

But although He was a king, this remarkable child was born in a most unremarkable place. For you see, the light of God's glory in the person of Jesus, that would one day be beheld by all men, first shone in a common stable, from a manger, the place of His birth. A picture, perhaps, of the fact that Jesus came to save all of us; small and great, (*Music starts.*) poor and rich; common and uncommon. Anyone can come and everyone is

welcome. Let's consider again that night when God's light came into the world.

Si - lent night!_____ ho - ly night!

Sleep in heav-en-ly peace.

Si - lent night!

ho - ly night, Shep - herds quake

Parts

love's pure light____ Ra - diant____ beams____ from

Thy ho-ly face, With the____ dawn of re -

deem - ing grace, Je - sus, Lord, at Thy

Tree Underscore

Music by MICHAEL FRAZIER
Arranged by Michael Frazier

NARRATOR: *(Music starts.)* I think most of us would agree, that some of the most wonderful things about Christmas are the

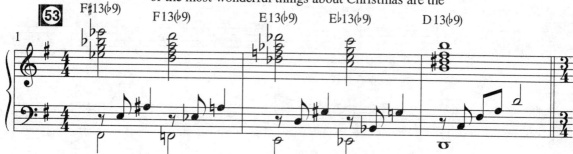

decorations. How many of us as children could hardly wait for mom or dad to get down the boxes marked Christmas, so we could again

take out our family treasures and display them proudly in their appropriate places. And of course, the centerpiece of it all was the Christmas tree,

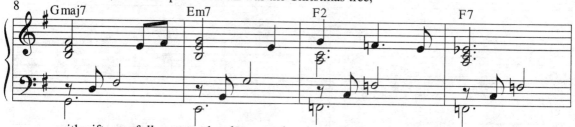

with gifts carefully wrapped and arranged underneath. But have you ever considered the rich spiritual symbolism that can be seen in the

Christmas tree? For instance, how an evergreen, speaks of God's eternal life and never ending love. The lights speak of the light of His truth and glory that shines through His Son.

Beneath The Tree Of Light

Words and Music by
PAULA CARPENTER & BILLY SIMON
Arranged by Michael Frazier and Dale Mathews

NARRATOR: The crimson ribbon is a powerful picture of the blood that flowed for us and of the life that was fastened to a tree for our sins. The ornaments represent the grace of God that adorns and brings His beauty to our lives. The gifts *(Music starts.)* that we give in honor of the lavish, extravagant gift of salvation in Jesus. Look carefully at the tree of light.

Let everything on it speak of God's incredible mercy in offering lost people a living Light that would lead them to Him.

can't be-lieve You love me like You do,___

60

lit - tle child at Christ - mas - time,— be - neath the tree— of light,— My—

Choir

Lit - tle child at Christ - mas - time,— be - neath the tree— of light,—

G · A/G · F♯m7 · Bm

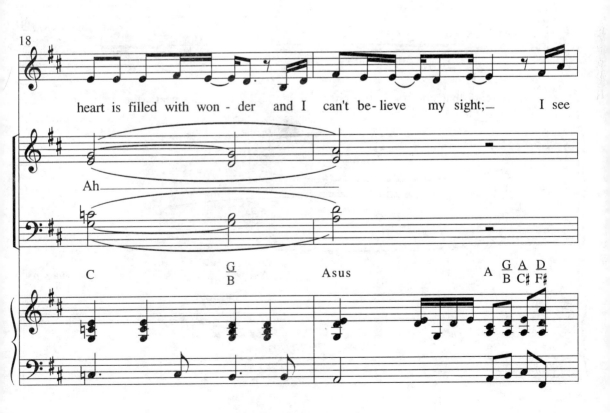

heart is filled with won - der and I can't be - lieve my sight;— I see

Ah—

C · G/B · Asus · A · G/B · A/C♯ · D/F♯

crim-son rib-bon flow - ing, sil - ver bells that hang— like tears,— And the

Crim-son rib-bon flow - ing, sil - ver bells that hang— like tears,—

pres-ents that por-tray the gift of life—— be-neath the tree of light.—

Ah—————

an-gel tops it all,— Like the le-gions that were watch-ing when Your

an-gel tops it all,— Like the le-gions that were watch-ing when Your

bod - y draped the cross,— As Your gift of life to us.—

bod - y draped the cross,— As Your gift of life to us,—

heart is filled with won - der and I can't be - lieve my sight;— I see

Ah

crim- son rib- bon flow - ing, sil - ver bells that hang— like tears,— And the

Crim- son rib- bon flow - ing, sil - ver bells that hang— like tears,—

pres-ents that por-tray the gift of life___ I'm like a

Ah___

lit-tle child at Christ-mas-time,___ be - neath the tree___ of light,___ My

Lit-tle child at Christ-mas-time,___ be - neath the tree___ of light,___

pres-ents that por-tray the gift of life___ be-neath the tree of light.___

Ah___

The tree of light,___

Crim-son rib-bon flow-ing___ on the tree of light,___

Follow Him Underscore

Music by MICHAEL FRAZIER
Arranged by Michael Frazier

NARRATOR: *(Music starts.)* As you consider the "tree of light" we hope that you are beginning to see just how much God loves you

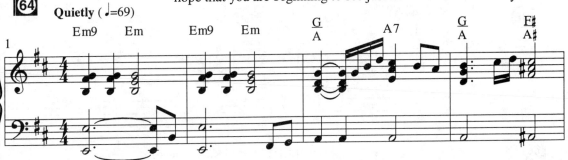

and just how much you can trust Him. For anyone who would love us and supply for us so completely would never do anything to hurt or destroy us. If we follow Him,

He will lead us into a bright tomorrow filled with hope and promise. When we follow the Lord's lead, He always makes us what we could never become on our own,

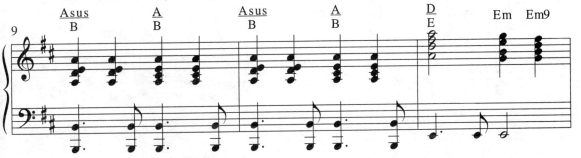

and gives us what we could never hope to obtain. As the shepherds came with haste to find Jesus in Bethlehem, and as wisemen traveled from afar to seek Him,

continue on

Follow Him / Lead Me, Lord

Arranged by Michael Frazier and Dale Mathews

NARRATOR: (cont.) so we should let go of anything that would hold us back and follow Him in faith and love. Lead us Lord, and we will follow.

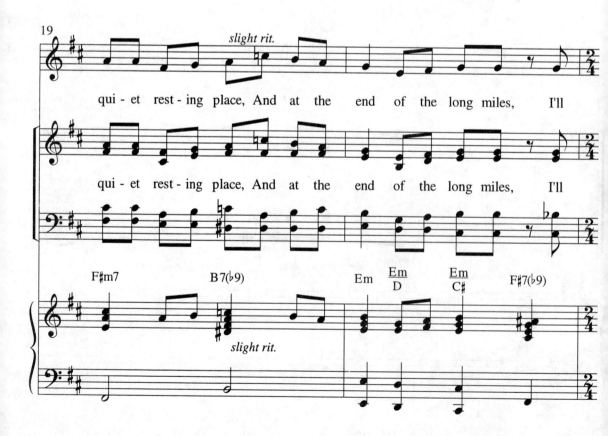

71 * LEAD ME, LORD (Wayne and Elizabeth Goodine)

Female solo

fol - low Him;   It's

fol - low Him;

hard to take the first step when I don't know the way, Each

turn is so un - cer - tain,— I learn to walk by faith;— But

Male solo   *Female solo*

You have called me, I will an - swer;   Lead me,

called me,   I will an - swer;

G   A   Bm   Bm/E   Em7

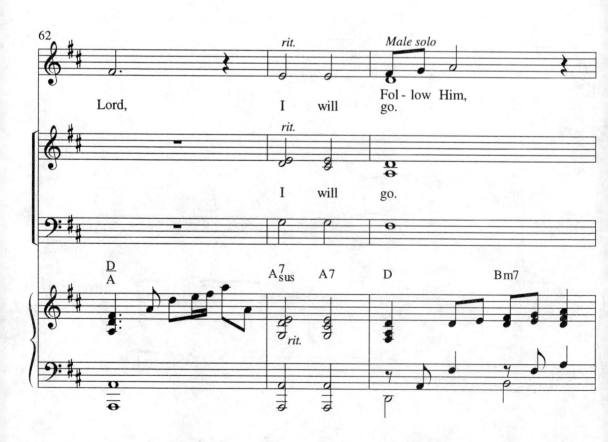

62   *rit.*   *Male solo*

Lord,   I   will   Fol - low Him,
                                              go.

rit.

I   will   go.

D/A   A7sus   A7   D   Bm7

rit.

some-thing in my heart keeps say-ing,——— "Fol-low Him;"

Lead me, Lord.———

Lead me, Lord.———

Lead Me, Lord
(A cappella)

Words and Music by
WAYNE and ELIZAGETH GOODINE
Arranged by Michael Frazier and Dale Mathews

Lead me, Lord, I will fol - low; Lead me, Lord, I will— go;___ You have called me, I will an - swer; Lead me, Lord, I will— go. You have called me, I will an - swer; Lead me, Lord, I will___ go.

Come Into My Heart, Lord

Words and Music by
WAYNE & ELIZABETH GOODINE
Arranged by Michael Frazier and Dale Mathews

NARRATOR: Most of us are familiar with the fact that Jesus was born in a stable because that was the only place that was open to Him. Today, Jesus is still looking for open places in human hearts where He can enter, bringing His light and life. One day, as Jesus was healing a man born blind, He declared, "I am the light of the world." At that same time Jesus was speaking to a group of people and said, "I have come that they may have life, and that they may have it more abundantly." Abundant light to see that abundant life could be found in Jesus. When Jesus comes, He always comes to conquer darkness and death and to replace them with abundant blessings. *(Music starts.)* Could we encourage you to make room for Jesus this Christmas. Some of us know Him, but have let life's cares crowd Him out. Others of us have never

opened to allow Him in. In either case, if you will open your life to Him,
He will offer His life to you.

hear the knock   most ev - 'ry day,   I   hear You gent - ly

(page 89, meas. 25)

Come, and live___ in me.

NARRATOR: Even now, Jesus is searching for people who will open their lives to Him. People who will trust Him as Savior and Lord.

That drawing that you are sensing is not the power of human persuasion. It is the Savior's love leading you to Himself.

Is there room in your heart for Jesus? Why not open your heart to Him in faith and let Him birth new life in you?

All you need to do is say, "Come into my heart, Lord. Be my Savior and my King."

Finale

Arranged by Michael Frazier and Dale Mathews

NARRATOR: *(Music starts.)* Christmas is a glorious celebration for those who know the joy of salvation that His coming brings. Christmas is also a loving invitation for those who seek Him, that they might know Him in the fullness of joy. We celebrate the beauty of Christmas in His light, the glory of Christmas through His life, and we receive the gift of Christmas through His love.

* JESUS, WHAT A WONDERFUL CHILD (Traditional)

glo - ry to the new - born King!

Glo - ry, glo - ry, glo - ry to the

new - born King!

O

* COME, LET US ADORE HIM (Dale Mathews)

Tree of Light
Production and Staging Notes
by Rhonda Frazier

Tree of Light can be effectively staged as a concert using a choir, soloists and narrator, or more elaborately produced with two sets, banners, multimedia display, costumes and nonspeaking cast members (or a combination of any of these ideas). The following production notes give you options for both types of production. Regardless of how you choose to stage the production, you will need a Christmas tree. Specific decorative elements should be used to portray the message of the musical. Refer to the "Beneath the Tree of Light" section for complete details.

As each section of the musical is discussed, the participants involved and items needed will be listed for easy reference.

A Note about the Narrator
The narrator's participation will be enhanced if he or she has memorized the narratives and talks to the audience instead of reading the script. If you have a lavalier microphone (wireless mic) and a follow spot, the narrator could walk around and be in different areas of the stage for each section. The production notes assume this is how you will be staging the musical and that this equipment is available. If you don't have a follow spot and a wireless mic, position the narrator stage left and use a stationary spot or lighting for each narrative.

You may want to consider asking your pastor to serve as narrator. There is a short sermon outline following the production notes that could be delivered seamlessly following "Come Into My Heart, Lord." However, the pastor may still come forward and deliver the invitational sermon even if he or she is not the narrator.

"Joy to the World"
The stage is black with choir in position upstage center. Bring up full lights on choir when music begins. *If you are using a live orchestra include them in the full lighting if their position allows for this.* Fade to black at end of song.

Narration 1 *(before Wonderful Counselor, page 13)*
Spotlight on narrator positioned stage left.

"Wonderful Counselor"
Bring up full lighting on choir at measure # 7, as narrator says "...that is the heart of the message of Christmas...."

Spotlight on the soloist. Full lighting remains on the choir.

Option 1: Banners

Banners offer a wonderful way to celebrate the attributes of our Lord. In "Wonderful Counselor," banners can be used to visually express the names of Jesus from Isaiah. If you are making your own banners, use one the following names on each:

Wonderful Counselor
Mighty God
Prince of Peace
Everlasting Father
Great I Am
King of the Ages
Emmanuel
King of Kings
Friend to the Friendless
Jesus or Jesus is His Name

If your church does not already have banners, contact your local Christian bookstore for references on making banners. Consider using the children of your church or the youth to help make the banners. Depending on the size of your banners the children or youth could be used to carry the banners. The banners can be elaborately decorated with gemstones, sequins and cutout lettering or they could be painted. The most important thing is that their beauty reflect the glory of God.

Bring the banners in at measure # 81, the beginning of the third chorus. Depending on the size of your church, you may need more or less time. Have the banners cross if possible at the very front of the church and keep them moving around the congregation until the end of the song when they should all be positioned across the front of the church. (The banners will be used again in the Finale.)

Option 2: Multimedia

Use slides of the names of Jesus. Consider enlisting the help of an artist from your congregation to draw the names or to write them in calligraphy. You could even consider using a computer program to print out the names. A local graphics company can assist you in making the slides if your church does not have that capability.

If you use the multimedia option, make eight slides of the name "Jesus." Begin the slides at the bridge, measure # 65. Each "Jesus" slide should be bigger and more elaborate than the last. Display a new slide each time the choir sings "Jesus." Then on the third chorus begin displaying the separate names of Jesus as they are sung.

Slide example:

Narration 2 *(Beautiful Name Underscore, page 27)*
Spotlight on narrator positioned center stage.

"Beautiful Name Medley"
Careful use of lighting will help to focus the musical on the intimate worship of this song after the flamboyant display of worship in "Wonderful Counselor."

Use a tight spotlight on the soloist to draw the congregation into the moment. Bring up low lights on the choir at the first chorus. At "We'll Call Him Jesus," the choir should be fully lit. Let the lights fade on the choir and bring the spot up on the narrator at stage left. After the narration, bring the lights up fully on the choir for "Come, Let Us Adore Him."

"Jesus, What a Wonderful Child"
This song is a celebration of the gift of Christ and the hope, joy and new life that He brings to all people. Use full lighting on the choir and soloist and consider them a unit for this song. If a live orchestra is positioned so they can be included in the lighting, feature them as well.

Narration 3 *(before Silent Night, page 51)*
Spotlight on narrator positioned stage right.

"Silent Night"
Use a nativity scene set up stage right, highlight with a soft spot. The set may be as simple as Mary, Joseph and the Baby in a manger, or as elaborate as the Family, plus shepherds, angels and a stable. The characters are to mime any action, allowing the text of the song to guide the action.

Narration 4 *(Tree Underscore, page 58)*
Tight spot on the narrator positioned stage left, but not a part of the scene.

Option 1: Family Room Set
Use a family room set stage left with the Christmas tree as the focal point of the room. The set can be as simple or elaborate as you wish to make it, however the following elements should be included: boxes marked "Christmas Decorations," a nativity set, ornaments to place on the tree.

This scene is a pantomime and can include as many characters as you wish. Consider using an actual family from your congregation. One "younger" child is necessary, however, because he or she will remain at the foot of the tree until the end of the song.

The characters should act out the actions being described by the narrator. This will move quickly so each participant should be ready to do his or her part. (Example: Place the nativity set on a table or on the mantle. Put an ornament or a red ribbon on the tree. Put a gift under the tree. Plug the tree in so that it lights up when the narrator says "centerpiece.") As the music begins, lights fade on the scene. All characters exit except for the youngest child who sits beneath the tree gazing up at it in awe.

Note: The soloist could be a part of the family unit. If so, the solo should be sung from the Family Room Set. If the soloist is a part of the scene, he or she should touch the tree and ornaments as the lyrics dictate.

Bring up soft lights on the choir at the chorus.

At the lyrics "When Your body draped the cross" use the special effect for the cross shadow that is described below along with the Christmas tree details.

Bring up full lights on the choir for the second chorus to the end.

At the end of the song fade to black except for the lit Christmas tree. The tree should remain lit for the remainder of the musical.

Option 2: Narrator and Christmas Tree

If you choose not to do the family room scene, have a large decorated tree with gifts underneath in place at stage left. The narrator can touch the tree and the ornaments as he or she speaks. Even using this method you still have the option to do the "cross special effect."

The Christmas Tree *(Needed regardless of which option you use!)*

The Christmas tree is essential to the musical. Use as large a tree as you can. ***Generously*** decorate the tree with the following items:

> white lights (nonblinking)
> lighted angel on the top
> red ribbons with long streamers (Make these if you can't purchase them.)
> silver bells (Spray paint will work if you can't find them in silver.)
> gold balls

Save one or two of the ornaments for the family to place on the tree if you're doing the family scene.

You will also need wrapped packages underneath the tree. Make these packages large and elaborate, just like Christ's gift to us.

Cross Special Effect

Some general guidelines are given here to accomplish a "shadow cross" behind the Christmas tree. Since each church building is different, specific sizes and distances cannot be given. This is something you will need to work out with your lighting and props.

The general idea is to cast a shadow of a cross behind the Christmas tree when the lyrics "when Your body draped the cross" are sung. Use a small spotlight positioned behind the Christmas tree and a wooden or cardboard cutout cross to make the shadow. The size of the cross and the distance it needs to be from the spotlight will depend on your particular dimensions. Timing is essential on this and depending on the wall the shadow will be cast on, you may need to use some sort of backdrop. Let the shadow remain on the wall until the end of the song. Cut the "cross" spot when the lights go to black at the end of the song. Only the Christmas tree remains lit.

Another option would be to place a screen behind the Christmas tree and at the appropriate time use a slide projector to display a slide of a cross. You could even display one with Christ on the cross.

Please remember that this effect needs to be experienced by the entire congregation, so casting a shadow that is big enough and clear enough is essential. This idea may take a little technical work and some extra rehearsal, but the final outcome is well worth the effort.

Narration 5 *(Follow Him Underscore, page 73)*
Spotlight on narrator as music underscore begins. Narrator is positioned at center stage. Christmas tree remains lit.

"Follow Him/Lead Me, Lord"
Spotlight on soloist positioned center stage right. Full lights up on choir when they come in at measure # 12. Spot on solo 1 fades and comes up on solo 2 positioned center stage left. Full lighting on choir and duet to end.

Narration 6 *(before Come Into My Heart, Lord, page 87)*
Spotlight on narrator positioned stage right.

"Come Into My Heart, Lord"
Consider interpretive movement or sign language to accompany this song. If you choose either of these options, have the soloist stand center stage right and the other participant positioned center stage left. If you decide to use interpretive movement, choose this participant early enough so that the music and movements are flowing out of a heart of worship. If you choose to use sign language, consult your local library or a nearby college or university for books, dictionaries or videos on American Sign Language.

Narration 7 *(middle of Come Into My Heart, Lord, page 90)*
This narration occurs during the song. Spotlight on narrator positioned stage right. If you are using any movement, the participant should be absolutely still during this section. If you are using sign language and the participant is proficient, consider signing this narrative section as well.

At the end of the narrative, bring the lights back up on all participants to finish the song.

ermon by Pastor

Here is the time for the suggested invitational sermon by the pastor. If he or she is serving s narrator the transition will be made easily. If the pastor is not the narrator, he or she hould step to center stage and begin the sermon as soon as the music stops. A sermon utline follows the production notes.

Narration 8 *(before Finale, page 93)*

Following the invitation by the pastor, the narrator moves to stage left for the final nderscored narration.

Finale"

f you used banners earlier, the finale gives you an opportunity to bring them back in for ne conclusion of your worship experience. Have the banners enter at the second chorus f "Come, Let Us Adore Him," measure # 62. (Depending on the size of your church and ne number of banners you have, you may need more or less time.) Have the banners ositioned across the front of the church by measure # 78. At this point have preselected nembers of the congregation rise and come forward to worship. *(People may kneel at the ltar, stand and raise hands in worship or simply join with the choir in singing, etc.)*

Choose a good representation of your congregation-- men, women, youth, children, niddle adults, seniors, etc. Decide who will be first, then let the other participants follow. This will be more dramatic, if the participants are scattered throughout the congregation, lthough place them near the aisles for easy access. This act of worship will also be more ffective if it is seen as a spontaneous response. In fact it would be great if persons rise nd come forward who have not been preselected!

Sermon Outline
by Pastor Dale Evrist
New Song Christian Fellowship, Brentwood, TN

By taking advantage of the imagery found in the decorated tree, a simple, yet very meaningful message very naturally presents itself:

1. **The Evergreen**: encourage people to open this morning/evening to God's gift of eternal life and never ending love. (John 3:16; 10:10; 20:31)

2. **The Lights**: Remind people that when Jesus came into the world He brought the light of God's truth and glory to be seen and understood by all men. (John 1:4-5; 1:14)

3. **The Crimson Ribbon**: share the fact that it was through the shed blood of Jesus, as He was nailed to a tree, that our sins could be paid for once and for all. (Col. 2:13-15)

4. **The Ornaments**: God's grace adorns and brings beauty to our lives. Encourage people that as they open to His grace, He will change their lives for the better. (Ps. 149:4, Isaiah 61:3)

5. **The Gifts**: bring people to a point of decision, asking them if they would like to receive the gift of salvation through faith in Jesus Christ. (Rom. 5:15-18, Eph. 2:8)

Note: The Pastor or whoever is doing the closing can use any other scriptures they would choose, as well as adding their own thoughts to this basic outline. I think that having a fully decorated tree in front of the church would be key for this outline to have the most impact.

COME INTO MY HEART, LORD

COME INTO MY HEART, LORD
WHERE YOU'RE LONGING TO BE
COME INTO MY HEART, LORD
COME AND LIVE IN ME

Words and Music by WAYNE & ELIZABETH GOODINE
© Copyright 1993 New Spring Publishing(ASCAP), a div. of Brentwood Music
Publishing, Inc. One Maryland Farms, Brentwood, TN 37027. All rights
reserved. Unauthorized duplication prohibited.

COME, LET US ADORE HIM

COME, LET US ADORE HIM
COME, BOW DOWN BEFORE HIM
COME, LET US WORSHIP HIM
JESUS, JESUS

GLORY SHINES ALL AROUND HIM
PEACE OF MIND ABOUNDS WHEN
WE COME TO WORSHIP HIM
JESUS, MY LORD

Words and Music by Dale Mathews